Report of an examination of the Bristol copper mine, in Bristol, Conn.,

Benjamin Silliman

[Printed for Private Distribution.]

REPORT

OF AN

EXAMINATION

OF THE

BRISTOL COPPER MINE,

IN

BRISTOL, CONN.,

BY

PROFESSORS B SILLIMAN, JR. AND J D. WHITNEY,

AUGUST, 1855.

NEW HAVEN.
PRINTED BY EZEKIEL HAYES
1855.

REPORT.

I. SITUATION AND REAL ESTATE.

This well known mine is situated in the north part of the town of Bristol, Connecticut, about three miles from the Canal Railroad, and four from the center of the town, where the depôt of the Hartford and Fishkill Railroad is located. It is, therefore, very easy of access and near to market. The freight to New Haven, by Railway, including hauling, is $2.40 per ton, and here most of the sales of ore have lately been made.

The real estate owned by the mine, in fee, is about 70 acres in one compact body, but the mining rights in a considerable tract beside, are held on easy terms.

The farm lands of the mine are good, and the farm is in good tilth. There is on the property a good dwelling house for the manager, besides cottages, an office, store and other buildings.

The water rights of a valuable stream are also owned by the mine, and the canal which brings it to the water wheels.

There is attached to the property an excellent peat swamp which will prove of great value for steam fuel in the proposed extension of the works.

An accurate map of the whole property has been lately prepared.

The persevering enterprise with which this mine has been explored, the rich character of its ores, the extent and costliness of its former workings, and the general impression, lately much strengthened, that it possesses still greater wealth in its ore-channels, all continue to make it a subject of peculiar interest to all who feel the national value of such investments and experience.

Its economical value is not diminished by the scientific interest attaching to the peculiarly complex nature of the deposit; but the full discussion of the questions connected with this portion of the subject, would be out of place in a report like this.

II. GEOLOGICAL POSITION AND NATURE OF THE DEPOSITS.

The Bristol Copper Mine is worked in a "contact deposit," between the sand-stone of the Connecticut River Valley, now supposed by geologists to be of Liassic age, and the older metamorphic rocks, commonly called primary, but in all probability of the palæozoic system.

The direction of the line of contact of the two formations at the mine is about N. E. and S. W.

The linear extent of ground known to be metalliferous, by excavations made at various times, is between 1100 and 1200 feet. The principal workings are, however, concentrated in a space of about 600 feet North and South. There is good reason to believe that the metalliferous ground does extend at least 1500 feet, and perhaps considerably further. The mine is opened to the depth of 40 fathoms (240 feet) by an engine shaft, 6'×8' in dimensions, sunk in the sand-stone, and passing out of this rock into the great ore-channel at this depth. This is at present the only working shaft of the mine, and is used for hoisting the ore for the pit work, and is closed road to the levels. The width of the ore-ground from East to West, or at right angles to the line of contact, at the entrance, it is exposed

TRANSVERSE SECTION OF BRISTOL COPPER MINE.

Showing the Contact of the Sandstone with the Crystalline Rocks, and the Position of the Great Flucan and Ore ground of the Mine.

Scale 60' to 1".

in the cross-cuts and levels which have been driven, is about 120 feet, and this width is maintained at the lowest depth yet reached in the mine, and the same is true for a longitudinal extent of about 500 feet, although it appears from the examination of the workings and what is known of their history, that the greatest concentration of metalliferous matter was near the surface in the vicinity of the engine shaft.

The character of the ore-ground or metalliferous belt is exceedingly complex.

Up to a recent period, however, the workings were chiefly in a series of micaceous and hornblende slates, sometimes passing into gneiss, and including large irregular "horses" of granite, which rock appears to have formed segregated masses, lying rudely parallel with the bedding of the schistose rocks. The strike and dip of these, however, is found throughout the mine to be very irregular, and there is evidence in the confused character of the ground, as well as in the slip joints and polished surfaces of the rocks, that motion of the various beds upon one another has taken place along lines of upheaval of limited extent and varying direction. The distribution of the ores in the metalliferous ground now under consideration, is found to be as irregular as is the structure of the ground itself. They consist principally of the vitreous, with some variegated ore, and a comparatively small amount of copper pyrites. The magnificent crystallizations found at the Bristol mine, especially of the vitreous ore, have given the locality a world-wide celebrity among mineralogists. In general these ores are found occurring in bunches and strings, which although preserving, usually, an approximate parallelism to the line of contact of the formations, cannot be traced continuously for any considerable distance. Hence the irregularity of the workings, especially in the upper levels, which have been extended in upon various branches of ore, or in search of others supposed to exist in certain directions, without any particular system or previously conceived plan. This has been the greatest drawback on the prosperity of the mine, since the orey ground was too wide to be all taken down by the miners, and the distribution of the branches of ore in it was too irregular to admit of their being found without occasional expensive excavations in dead ground. In general, throughout the mine, a tendency to a concentration of the ore around the masses of granite may be remarked, and the latter are not unfrequently well filled with strings and bunches of ore, especially near their exterior.

The limits of the ore ground to the West, or in the direction of the older rocks, the sandstone being to the East of the contact-line, have never been well ascertained, and must be somewhat irregular, as would be expected from the nature of the deposit. Eustis's level, going North from the 20-fathom crosscut, has been driven along a well marked and regular wall, which has been commonly called the foot wall of the mine. This dips, at an angel of 62° to the East, preserving a very near parallelism with the line of contact of the formations. The same kind of wall is seen in the 30-fathom level immediately beneath, where it is observed in the 20, but in neither level can it be traced for more than one or two hundred feet. There is nothing in the nature of the wall to indicate that ore might not be found beyond it as appearances similar to this are observed in the ore-bearing ground of the mine. The excavations indicate that there was a tendency of the metalliferous matter towards this limit, and that there is not much probability of finding large bunches of ore beyond it. It is worthy of remark, however, regarding the ore ground within the limits just described, that the average distribution of the vitreous copper is very uniform, so much so that for a long period it has been found profitable to crush and work over nearly every stone from this belt raised in working the mine.

The ore-ground just described was from the time the mine was first opened up to a recent period, considered as the only source in which the yield of copper was to be sought. Not long since, however, attention began to be called to a belt of soft rock, which lies next adjacent to the sandstone, and, of course, between it and the metalliferous belt just described. This belt is known as the "great flucan," (see diagram,) and it consists of a talco-micaceous slate, completely disintegrated and softened by some chemical agency, with the exception of a few bands and nodules of hard rock, but which are of very limited extent compared with the softer portion. The flucan contains throughout its whole mass vitreous and other ores of copper, usually disseminated through it in small particles, so as hardly to be visible to the naked eye, but occasionally concentrated into bunches and strings of considerable size. The width of the great flucan is 27 feet in the 20-fathom level, but it increases rapidly as the workings descend, being respectively 38 and over 50 feet, in the 30 and 40-fathom level. If this increase in width were to continue in depth, the flucan will meet the so called foot-wall of the mine at or near the 80 fathom level, occupying in this place a width of about 120 feet. But that such an increase in its dimensions continues downwards indefinitely, seems hardly probable, it is more likely that it will be found to be a lenticular mass swelling out to great dimensions, and then gradually contracting again. The mass of flucan has been traced on the surface and opened at various points. At the distance of 700′ to the Southwest, from the engine-shaft it has near the surface an inconsiderable width, although it may increase in descending: to the North, however, it holds its width as far as it has been explored. Jilbard's level was driven in this direction from the 20-fathom cross-cut, for a distance of over 300 feet, and the flucan there found to have a width of 41 feet. Still further to the North it has been cut at the surface, beyond Ives's level, but its width in this place was found to be at 30 feet from the surface much diminished

The deposits of ore are not entirely confined to the primary Within the sandstone, which at the line of junction is so broken up and irregular, that its stratification can with difficulty be made out, a small seam of ore was cut in the 20-fathom cross cut from the engine shaft. It has been driven on both ways from the cross cut to a distance of about 160 feet to the North, and 120 to the South The upper part of this course of ore is still standing, showing a narrow seam of quartz rich in ore. The level to the North is at present inaccessible to the South the ore appears to run out at a distance of about fifty feet from the cross cut (This seam of ore is shown in the cross section at A)

III HISTORY OF THE MINE

This locality has been known for a long period as a place furnishing copper, and was opened to a very limited extent many years since In 1836 Mr G W Bartholomew made an open cut in a spot where indications of ore were abundant, and the following account of its appearance is given in 1837, by Prof C U Shepard, State Geologist, who saw it at that time:

"The trench has a nearly North and South course, and extends for twenty feet somewhat obliquely across alternations of vertical layers of granite and soft mica slate. The layers of granite are from one to two feet in thickness, while those of the slate are generally much less It was found on getting below the surface that the green malachite and brown iron ochre diminished in quantity, and that the rocks were less decomposed Yellow copper pyrites began to make its appearance in the slate and variegated copper in the granite The integrity of the rocks and the abundance of the ore increased regularly as the workmen descended, till at the bottom the granite presented several almost continuous veins or layers of ore which in places had a thickness of two inches."—*Report*, p. 47.

Mr Percival says: "The Bristol Mine is chiefly opened in a large vein of a coarse reddish sub-talcose granite, adjoining which the gneissoid micaceous rock, just referred to, is also sub talcose or sub-chloritic, with decomposed greenish chloritic seams and nodules, and with more or less copper disseminated."—*Report*, p. 77.

The property subsequently passed into the hands of Mr A. R. Miller, who drove various shallow levels near the surface, exploring for copper. While in his possession it was visited and reported on by Prof Silliman, Senior, of Yale College, in 1839. and upon this report funds, to a small amount, were obtained in England for prosecuting the work.* But the adventurers being unable to sustain the enterprise, the explorations were subsequently continued by Mr L C Ives, who erected a small steam engine, and sunk the present engine shaft in the sandstone to the 20-fathom level. During this time, and prior to 1847, considerable shipments of the ore had been made to England, but exactly what quantity we have no means of ascertaining It appears, however, from the information obtained from the last named proprietor, that it could not have been less than 100 to 125 tons.

It was not, however, until 1846-7, that the mine was opened and worked to any considerable extent. At that time it passed into the hands of Mr Hezekiah Bradford and his associates Since that period a large amount of money has been expended here and over eighteen hundred tons of copper ore have been raised and sold. In 1851 the management of the mine passed into the hands of Mr. Henry H Sheldon, as agent for the present owners. Mr. Sheldon (who is still the manager) has had

---

* This Report was in confirmation of one made in October, 1838, by Prof C U Shepard, and which we have never seen

the satisfaction of seeing the mine rise from a state of great depression in its affairs and prospects to a condition of prosperity and encouraging profits, with the certainty that by a judicious and moderate outlay, it can be made to return the whole cost of its plant and extraordinary expenses, with a wide margin of profit to the adventure. In addition to this it is our conviction that the hope of future discoveries of great value in the continued exploration of the mine, was never more allied to certainty in any similar enterprise.

The following statement, taken from the books of the mine, shows for what classes of expense the money has been used:

EXPENDITURE AT THE BRISTOL MINE FROM 1846 TO MAY 1st, 1855.

For Land and Leases,	$128,253 94
Buildings,	16,761 08
Ore Dressing Machinery,	28,891 77
Mining Machinery,	28,395 75
Water Power,	11,821 72
Tools,	8,999 83
Machine and building for dressing ore by wind,	8,428 25
Underground labor,	98,090 77
Dressing ore, (surface men,)	64,687 25
Underground materials,	11,330 07
Horses, wagons and carriages, including expenses of Stable and Ostlers' wages,	10,030 89
Traveling expenses,	5,501 85
Fuel,	9,356 45
Salaries, and unapportioned labor,	16,559 07
Miscellaneous,	10,168 78
Total,	$190,310 17

From these figures, it appears that, in round numbers, there has been expended for mine and plant, about $200,000 00

For mining expenses, including raising and dressing
ore, about $175,000 00

leaving about $115,000, which has been consumed in a variety of ways.

The avails from ore raised to the same date, May 1st, (viz $186,582 08,) have but little more than covered the actual mining and ore dressing expenditures. We propose, therefore, having given its geological position, to go into an examination of the mine, its method of working and present condition, with a view to ascertain, as far as possible, what its real value is, and how large a portion of the expenditures which have been made here, may be considered as having been legitimately applied to opening the mine, and how far the excess of expenditure over the receipts may be considered as having been necessitated by the character of the mine itself. We shall also attempt to show that the true nature of the mine was never understood until quite a recent period,* and that its future success is predicated upon our present knowledge of that character.

The ore sold from Bristol mine from 1847 up to the first of August, 1855, amounting to 1811 tons (of 2352 lbs) is exhibited in the annexed table drawn from the account sales of the mine

TABLE OF PRODUCE OF BRISTOL COPPER MINE.

Year	Ore Sold		Per centage yield of Ore			Average	Amount
	Tons	Pounds	Highest	Lowest	Average	value per ton	received
1847,	128	279	50 75	21 23	41 13	147.01	
1848,	583	837	48 00	14 78	31.76	103 15	
1849,	365	717	48 73	37 25	41 67	146 99	
1850,	161	1950	44 40	17 18	30 80	98 56	
1851,	49	1966	19 67	15 00	17 55	48 28	
1852,	32	646	29 80	29 37	29 58	100.50	
1853,	135	865	38 00	16.10	27 41	107 55	
1854,	189	430	38 22	21 00	27 33	136 03	
1855 (6 m ths)	166	781	31 55	21 26	27 00	118 84	
Totals,	1811	1415	38 57	21 46	30·80		$197 420

* It is noteworthy that the State Geologists do not allude to the important fact that this mine is on the line of contact of the two formations.

IV. THE PRESENT POSITION OF THE MINE

Since the introduction of the Bradford separators and the systematic workings of the great flucan, the mine has returned handsome monthly profits. It is safe to state these profits as about $1800 per month, over all expenses.

The average monthly expenses are now about $2,250, including repairs of and additions to machinery, and the salary of the Manager. The expenses for the month of July last, gives us a fair specimen of the items which make up this cost. We copy from the Journal.

Underground Labor,		$799 66	
"	Materials,	17 90	
"	Timber,	23 38	
"	Candles,	30 99	
"	Machinery,	118 73	
	Total Underground Cost,		$990 66
Surface	Dressing Ore,	$708 30	
	Dressing Machinery, (repairs,)	92 44	
	Wood for Steam Engine,	80 00	
	Total Surface Expenses,		$880 94
Miscellaneous,	Assaying,	$25 00	
	Jobbing 5 04, Stable 30 00,	35 04	
	Store Keeper,	30 00	
	Oil,	49 29	
	Salary Manager,	140 00	
			379 33
	Total Expenses for July,		$2,250 93

The average yield of ore per month is 30 tons, which at $135 per ton, present price, is equal to $4,050, being a profit of $1800 over the expenses. The present limited machinery and shaft are now worked to their full capacity both day and night.

In determining, therefore, the practicability of increasing the present product of the mine to an amount which will speedily return the former cost of the plant and leave a profit for the adventurers, it becomes requisite to examine critically the resources of the mine as *at present known*

V. RESOURCES OF THE MINE

We have already described the geological position of the ascertained ore ground of the mine. Its resources are comprised under the following items viz:

1. Value of the great flucan, within ascertained limits
2. " " ore in the crystalline rocks
3. " " ore in the sandstone
4. " " Halvans on Surface
5. " " Raft on Surface
6. " " the real estate and plant of the mine.

We will consider these several items separately and then make a summary of the results

1. *Value of the flucan.*—The width and extent of this ore channel have been already described. It has now been the subject of long continued and successful exploration, and so many assays and mining "vans" have been made of its contents, that we are no longer in doubt as to the approximate amount of its metallic contents, especially as the whole product of the mine has now been derived from it for two years, and the records of the smelter show that the value predicated upon it is actually obtained in practical working *

---

* The fact that the flucan contained ore was not overlooked by the former managers of this mine, but it was supposed to be impracticable either to take it down safely or to work it with profit. The new modes of mining and dressing,—in which the Bradford Separators serve a most important purpose—have now rendered this an easy and certain operation

The average of thirteen humid assays of the flucan taken from the various levels and cross-cuts made by Mr. Stadtmuller in 1853, show 1.103 per cent of metallic copper, or about 3.67 per cent. of 30 per cent. ore. Fourteen assays of samples collected by ourselves in May of this year, show an average of 2.65 per cent. of ore, as may be seen in detail in the annexed table.

Locality of Samples, of which 1840 or 5,760 grs. was vanned	Weight of Ore obtained by Van	Percentage of Ore obtained	Metallic Copper obtained by assay
GREAT FLUCAN NORTH RUN. (20 fathom level)			
do do	5¼ dwts	2.29	24.60
do do	4¼ "	2.85	21.92
do do	211 grs	1.02	11.64
do do	5¼ "	2.29	2.98
do do	9.6 "	5.78	44.63
SOUTH (20 fathom level)			
Foot of Ladder in winze,	6.15 "	1.14	35.36
do another,	4 "	2.49	30.00
Cross cut,	4.11 "	2.78	21.01
Davy's level S of cross cut	4.12 "	3.90	31.47
do do do	3.11 "	1.95	19.19
Cross cut in sand-tone,	6 "	2.50	.505
Bottom and cross cut,	3.3 "	1.20	40.76
Another do	.1 "	1.26	14.97
Averages		2.57	28.08

Ten humid assays by Mr. Storm, the present mine assayer, of the weekly averages of the work done by the crushers and stamps in July and August of the present year, show an average richness of 1.17 per cent. metallic copper, equal to 3.90 per cent. of 30 per cent. ore.

The weekly averages of the results of stamping and crushing are obtained from small hourly portions of stuff put aside by the attendants on each of these processes. These quantities are then carefully sampled by the captain of the mine, and a weighed quantity of each is subjected to the "van."* Such an average is plainly much more perfect than any other that can be

---

* The term is applied to the method of washing ores on a shovel, called a *van miny shovel* and in which operation a skillful miner can usually obtain better results than are obtained by the best ore dressing machinery.

obtained. The results of these trials for the 22 weeks ending August 13th, give the following:

Average from the crushers, 3.04 per cent. of 30 p. c. ore.
Average from the stamps, 2.32

Mean of the two, . . 2.68

The summary of all these modes of trial is as follows:

By Stadtmuller in 1853, . 3.66
By ourselves in 1855, . . 2.65
By mine assay, " . . 3.90
By captain's van, { Crushers, 3.04
{ Stamps, 2.34
Mean of the five modes, . 3.11 per cent of 30 p. c. ore

This average of ore is equal to $\frac{103}{110}$th of one per cent. of metallic copper in the fluean. But as all the ore cannot be obtained by washing, even with the present improved modes, we will reduce the probable yield to 2.5 per cent of 30 per cent ore. This amount will undoubtedly continue to be realized in working on the large scale, as it has been heretofore. The ore actually sold this year returns $2\frac{51}{100}$ per cent. to the whole amount of stuff worked over, which is a surprisingly close approximation to the calculation just made, and to the average of the captain's vans.*

---

* Some persons who may see this Report may be surprised that a mine can be worked at a large profit whose ores are of so low a percentage. It is well, therefore, to make a few comparative statements.

The yield of the Copper Mines worked so extensively in Russia, in the Permian Rocks, is only 2¼ per cent of ore. The mines of Mansfeld in Prussia, yielding a large profit, contain a much smaller per cent than this.

The whole copper ores sold in Cornwall for 1854 were about 180,000 tons, yielding some 11,000 tons of fine copper, or about 6.5 per cent metal to the ores sold after *they were dressed for smelting*, and for the month of June, 1855, the average richness of the dressed ores was only 5 per cent. As the Bristol ores are dressed at 30 per cent from an ore stuff equal to a little less than one per cent of metallic

Estimate, then, a body of this ore-ground actually seen and measured, as 500 feet long, 33 feet average width and 240 feet deep, and weighing by trial 150 pounds to the cubic foot, and we have a total weight of rock, of 252,551 miners' tons of stuff, yielding equal to 6,313 tons of 30 per cent. ore. This at present prices, $135.00 per ton, will yield . . $852,255.00

Less, mining and dressing and all expenses, at $1 40 per ton on 252,551 tons,* . . . $353,571.40

Leaving for net avails from flucan, . . $498,683 60

2 & 3 The value of the ore in the crystalline rocks or in the wide belt of ore ground adjacent to the flucan, and already described, it is impossible to estimate accurately. As the flucan is withdrawn, the old arches now standing over the galleries and passages of the mine will fall, and be brought up in rich fragments, as is the case at present daily. Many rich spots for exploration have been noted in our survey under ground, which in the continued working of the mine will all come to surface. the Manager and the Mining Captain express the conviction, that as much ore remains now standing in this ground as has

---

copper, some notion may be formed of the low percentage of the whole ore staff moved to obtain the British ores which are dressed only to 5 or 6 per cent. And yet the Cornish Copper Mines last year divided over $10,000,000 of profits on the year's business. It should also be remembered, that the vitreous and variegated ores of copper, which are the ores of B M, contain respectively 79 and 69 parts of copper in the hundred parts, while yellow copper, (the prevailing ore of Cornwall,) if pure, contains but 34 to

* The present cost of mining and dressing, with the absence of tram roads below and on the surface and other conveniences for economical management has been about $1 80 per ton. A careful calculation of the cost of mining with the proposed improved facilities, shows that it may be done, if three fold the present quantity is mined, all told, for $1 37 per ton. If four fold the present business is done, the expense will probably be even less than that, but we have adopted the above sum ($1 40) as a safe and reliable one

been formerly taken out; and on that supposition have estimated the returns of this portion of the mine at $200,000, and the vein in the sandstone at $15,000. While we cannot add these items to our estimate of the resources of Bristol Mine with the same certainty as in the case of the flucan, it is quite safe to express our conviction that there will be great returns from this portion of the ore ground. Probably the net avails from these sources should reach $100,000 above the 40-fathom level

4. *The halvans.*—During the early history of the present enterprise, and when the dressing machinery was very imperfect, much ore was rejected, which can now be worked over to a good profit. Very large accumulations of this material exist on the surface, and from a superficial measurement and the explorations we have caused to be made in sinking a shaft in the heap, we assume this material will probably return net $15,000.*

5. *The raft.*—A survey of the vast raft heaps (the result of former ore dressings) on the south of the present works shows that they contain about 6,300 miners' tons of material, all in a state of fine division and impregnated with copper. Fortunately we are not left to conjecture as to the probable value of this accumulation of the refuse of former workings. We possess over one hundred assays made, sometimes daily, during 1849 and 1850, by Mr Stadtmuller, former assayer to the mine. The average of all these assays gives us $1\frac{55}{100}$ per cent. metallic copper for the whole equal to $325\frac{1}{4}$ tons of 30 per cent ore, worth over $45,000. As the material is already on the surface and in condition to be economically dressed, the expense of working it over will not exceed by calculation 35 cents per ton

---

* This estimate rests on an area of 150 feet diameter and 10 feet deep of stuff of the same richness as the flucan. It will, from present appearances, exceed the flucan in richness.

By comparing the earlier and later assays of this raft it will be seen that as the means of dressing ore was improved, the raft became poorer. Thus in 1849 it was for the year 2.61 per cent. copper, and on the 27th of October, 1849, it was 5.32, while in 1850 it averaged 1.51 per cent. In the year of greatest productiveness of the mine (1848) there were no assays of the raft.

In this estimate no account has been taken of the value of the material now on the old dressing floors and accumulated in various ways and to a notable depth about the present buildings all of which will, in the proposed new arrangements, be profitably worked over. We set the probable value of the raft and of the the surface waste at $40,000 net

We have then the following summary of the resources of the Bristol Mine in ore after deducting the expenses of working, &c

1	Value of the Flucan,	. . .	$498,653 60
2 & 3	" " other ore ground.	.	100,000 00
4.	" " Halvans,	. . . .	15,000 00
5	" " Raft, &c,	. .	40,000 00
			$653,653 60
6	" " Plant of the mine, estimated as		200,000 00
	Total.	. . .	$853,653.60

It will be seen that this estimate takes no account of the discovery of new deposits of ore in future explorations, nor of the continuance of the flucan and other ore ground in depth. Although it is in the highest degree probable that the exploration of this deposit to the hundredth fathom will confirm our opinion in its continued richness, we will not permit this circumstance to affect our estimate, the object of which is to show that there is ore enough in sight to authorize placing the mine without delay upon new basis of sufficient extent to enable its proprietors to realize most satisfactory returns.*

VI. BRADFORD'S SEPARATORS

As the present and future success in working Bristol Mine are closely dependent on the use of new and improved machinery, of which the ore separators of Mr. H. Bradford form an important part, it becomes interesting to examine with critical care, the operation of these machines, as exhibited in the experience of this mine since February last. The results of these operations, as well as those of the whole mine, are accurately registered at the close of every week and tabulated in printed forms

From the 17th of February to the 21st of April, (11 weeks,) when only seventeen of the machines were in action, 78,201 pounds of ore were separated by them in $1,378\frac{11}{100}$ hours This makes the hourly product of each machine $3\frac{103}{1000}$ pounds or $79\frac{272}{1000}$ pounds for a full day of 24 hours

From the 22nd of April to the 28th of July, (13 weeks,) 18 machines produced 102,925 pounds of ore in $1,723\frac{1}{4}$ hours running time The hourly produce of each machine for this period was therefore $3\frac{243}{1000}$ pounds of ore, or for the full day $77\frac{832}{1000}$th pounds. The average of these two products is $78\frac{55}{100}$ pounds per day for each machine, if full time was run, of ore estimated at 30 per cent

There was however a loss of 6 per cent of time on the first period, and of 7 per cent on the second, and the product of the machines is therefore subject to a like deduction

---

* A statement has been circulated in the public prints that the discovery of a new deposit of ore had been made at Bristol valued at one million of dollars This statement is, no doubt, founded upon the testimony given before the Legislative Committee in May, that there were probably over a million dollars worth of ore now standing in the mine. If the *gross* sums just enumerated are added up, it will be seen that this statement is confirmed

The absolute or actual average for each machine was therefore for the first period of 11 weeks, $73.\frac{784}{1000}$ pounds, and for the second period of 13 weeks, $74.\frac{546}{1000}$ pounds. Mean for the whole time of 24 weeks, 74 pounds of ore daily for each machine.

The whole amount of stuff dressed upon the separators is obtained indirectly as follows. The total weight of ore stuff dressed during 122 days, as drawn from the records, was 11,918,900 pounds of rock stamped and crushed, or 5,080 tons miner's weight. The total ore sold from this quantity of stuff, was 128 gross tons (2,352 lbs.) or $2\frac{41}{100}$ per cent. of the stuff worked over. By the Captain's vans the average richness of the stamp work (forming much the larger part of what goes to the separators,) for 22 weeks was 2.32 per cent. The humid assay of the average work from the stamps for five weeks in July and August gave for the richness of the stuff dressed on the separators 3.28 per cent. of ore, or .984 per cent. of metallic copper. There is therefore an apparent loss in the tailings of $\frac{77}{100}$ per cent. of 30 per cent. ore or $\frac{23}{100}$th of copper. The amount of ore however lost in the tailings, does not exceed $\frac{5}{10}$ to $\frac{6}{10}$ per cent. or about $\frac{15}{100}$th per cent. of copper. The actual products of working, therefore, as may be seen exceed for the machines, the average richness of the Captain's vans.

Of the total ore produced in this time, 181,126 pounds came from the separators and 160,858 pounds from the jiggers. The whole amount of stuff therefore required to produce this amount of ore, estimated from the above ratio (1.15 : 1) is 7,686,80 pounds. This may be taken approximately as the actual quantity which passed over the separators, and if calculated on the Captain's vans, it should have produced 177,961 pounds of ore, while in fact it did produce 181,126 pounds of ore, a truly remarkable coincidence, being in fact a variation in excess for machines of only 3,210 pounds. Each of the separators therefore dresses about 1½ tons of rock daily, of stuff yielding an average of 2.5 per cent. of 30 per cent. ore.

Undoubtedly Bradford's separators are the most important mechanical invention ever produced for dressing what are called slime ores. The principle upon which they are constructed is truly philosophical, and has been most ingeniously applied by the talented inventor to the production of this machine. Like all accurate instruments they require careful adjustment in all particulars; but once adjusted they are completely self-acting, so that one attendant can easily oversee at least twenty of them.

VII. PRESENT SURFACE ARRANGEMENTS AND DRESSING MACHINERY.

The only motive power employed about this mine is water, with the exception of a single horizontal high pressure engine of six horse power, which is used exclusively for working the eighteen Bradford separators and the necessary elevating and other machinery attached to them.

The water power is derived from a small stream to the Northwest of the mine, from which the water is brought by a canal four-fifths of a mile in length. There are two wheels, the water being used twice. The upper one is near the engine shaft, and is 32' in diameter, and 6' breast. This wheel is used to drive the crushers and stamps and for hoisting the ore. The lower one is 34' in diameter and 12' breast, and is employed for pumping at the engine shaft, the power being conveyed to the shaft by a flat rod 1300 feet in length and running on friction rollers. Both wheels are in good order; the lower one was built in 1853, in the most substantial manner and is well housed. The supply of water is abundant except during the Summer months, when, if the season is dry, the power is not usually sufficient to move all the machinery at once. There appears to be no available supply of water to make good this deficiency, and auxiliary steam power must be resorted to for this purpose, and will, at all events, be necessary in case of any increase on the quantity of machinery now in operation.

The ore is hoisted by a whim of a form of construction believed to be peculiar to this mine. The power is applied to an endless screw by means of friction wheels, so contrived as to admit of instantaneous reversal, without any change of motion on the part of the driving machinery. On arriving at the surface, the ore is divided into two classes—the soft flucan and disintegrated rock goes to the stamps, the fragments and masses of solid rock containing disseminated particles of ore are destined for the crushers. If the whole contents of the kibble belong to the first class, they are dumped into a wagon at an elevated landing, and conveyed on a tram road to the stamps a distance of about 100′. If the kibble contains mixed flucan and solid rock, the contents are shot on to a dressing floor; the soft part is separated by a man in attendance, and conveyed to the stamps; the remainder is thrown on to the crusher after having been spalled or broken in fragments of suitable size. There are two crushers in use; the first one breaks the fragments into pieces of the size of the fist; the second reduces them to a coarse powder; for which purpose the stuff as it passes the crusher is screened, the coarser portion, or that which does not pass through the meshes being conveyed by an elevator back to the crushers, while the finer particles are raised to a higher floor, where they are mixed with water and then screened. The size of the meshes of this screen is 10 to the inch, and all that does not go through these meshes is separated by jigging, while that which does pass them is mixed with the slime from the stamps and goes to the Bradford machines. The jigs are four in number, and are worked by hand.

There are four batteries of stamps of five heads each, the stamp head and beam weighing about 400 lbs each. The gratings have ten apertures to the inch. The stuff as it passes through them is moved by an Archimedean screw in the direction of an elevator, which takes it up to the screens. These are two in number, 22 and 60 holes to the inch, and assort the material for the Bradford separators, eighteen of which are now in use.*

VIII. PROPOSED PLAN OF FUTURE OPERATIONS.

From the statistics of the mine and the facts and arguments of this report, we advise the following course for the future, in order to develop fully the productive capacity of the property.

1. The erection of new works on the ground East of the present works, and on a scale capable of working over at least four times the present quantity of ore stuff.

2. In order to supply this increased quantity of material, to explore the flucan in depth, and to drain the mine, it will be necessary to sink a new engine shaft far enough to the East, upon the sandstone, to cut the flucan at the 80th or 100th-fathom, and in such a position as to be out of reach of all cracks and fissures produced from working the flucan in depth. Also to sink at least one whim shaft, somewhere in the vicinity of the adit level on Ive's lode, and on the underlie of the foot-wall, from which ore stuff can be supplied to the machinery before the engine shaft is in a position to return ores. To economize labor, the stuff must be raised in iron wagons of about one ton capacity, which are made to traverse tram roads, both under ground and over the surface, and the stuff must be dumped at such an elevation that it will descend by gravity to the crushers, stamps and other dressing machinery.

3. Steam power will be required to carry the new machinery. The upper water wheel can be kept in action only until the new machinery is ready, since all the surplus water now owned by the mine, and not required by the lower or pumping wheel, will be demanded by the greatly increased number of stamps, separators and other machinery.

---

* A new form of jig invented also by Mr Bradford has just been put to work at Bristol, and so far as it has been tried, has yielded the most satisfactory results September 10

A parallel motion cornish condensing engine of about 36" cylinder, 7' stroke will be required to do the work, and to furnish auxiliary power to the pumps during the dry months of summer. The peat of the swamp adjacent the mine should be systematically worked by a coffer dam and machine pumps, and will furnish excellent fuel at a moderate cost.

4. The present system and machinery of the mine must be kept up until the first section of the new works are in full operation, when the machinery now in use can be transferred to its proper place in the new works.

5. The raft and the halvans can be most economically dressed in the new machinery, and will furnish material sufficient to occupy it for several months until the proposed new shaft can be made to return ores. The raft can be successfully ground in burr stones, either with or without water. But as this mode of preparing ores is a novelty, we recommend that a pair of 4½' Harrison's patent stones be added to the present machinery, and run upon the raft until by sufficient experience the feasibility of this plan is tested.

6. We advise the adoption of one of the plans for the arrangement of the machinery drawn by Mr Richardson, and preferably the one which, with the greatest compactness of form admits of the erection of works in successive order, as the development of the mine may require.

7. Miners' cottages, a boarding house for work people, a school house, to be used for worship on Sunday, and a new carpenter shop, with power, are amongst the earliest things required to be done before the contemplated plans can be realized.

IN RESUME.

In reviewing the condition of the Bristol Mine at the present time, the following are the most noteworthy points:

1. The mine is one of the few in the United States which is now worked at a profit.

2 There is a large extent of ore-ground known to exist in the mine, and which can, although of a low percentage of ores, be worked to a profit.

3 There is good stoping ground in the solid parts of the mine, which can be profitably wrought.

4. The widening of the flucan in descending, and the appearance of the solid ore ground at the lowest points yet reached by the workings, render it a safe and advisable matter to open the mine at a considerably greater depth. Since there it is certain that the flucan may be wrought with profit, and there is good reason to believe that good leaders of ore will be cut in the solid part of the ground, and to hope that the various branches may unite into one master lode or form rich bunches of ore at the crossings of the East and West branches

5 The position of the dressing works is such in relation to unsettled ground, that their position must be changed, or prepations made for doing so immediately.

6. A new engine shaft must be commenced to cut the lode at 80 or 100 fathoms, and must be pushed forward as rapidly as possible.

7. The ore stuff now on the surface will go far towards returning the cost of all necessary improvements requisite to place the mine in a state of great productiveness, and with proper care the old works can be kept up with undiminished returns during the erection of the new machinery

All which is respectfully submitted by your obedient servants,

BENJAMIN SILLIMAN, Jr,
Professor of General and Applied Chemistry in Yale College

J D WHITNEY
State Geologist of Iowa

Bristol, August 26th, 1855,

APPENDIX.

Since the above date, Experiments have been made at the Bristol mine, in the use of Bradford's jigs, (of which mention has been made on page 24) which promise to be of great importance in the economy of time and labor in ore dressing It is found that when the whole product of crushing or stamping is fed to these machines that a concentration of the metallic sulphurets is made to such an extent, that nine-tenths of the whole weight of raw material is passed off as a valueless waste, while all the ore is obtained in one-tenth which is collected in the Hutch with a portion of fine sand in a state to be very easily raised to a high percentage on the Separators. The abridgment of labor and cost in mining by this mode of proceeding is very important, and can be easily appreciated by those who are familiar with ore dressing processes This jig is fed by a steady stream of water conveying ore, and its construction is such as to permit the waste to pass off continuously on one side through apertures provided for it while the ore collects in the Hutch For this purpose the Hutch is divided into two compartments by a vertical division, of which one side of the screen box forms a part This jig is operated by machinery

Nov 20, 1855

CHARTER

OF

THE BRISTOL MINING COMPANY.

GENERAL ASSEMBLY, MAY SESSION, 1849.

Resolved by this Assembly,

SEC. 1. That James Brown, Horatio Allen, Robert M. Stratton, Edward C. Delevan, Erastus Corning and John T. Norton, with all others who are or shall hereafter become associated with them, be, and they hereby are, with their successors and assigns, made and established a body politic and corporate, by the name of "*The Bristol Mining Company,*" for the purpose of mining, for smelting and vending ore, minerals, earths and metallic substances of every description, in the most advantageous manner,—and by that name they and their assigns and successors shall be, and hereby are authorized and empowered to purchase, take, hold, occupy, possess and enjoy, to them and their successors, any goods, chattels and effects of whatever kind they may be, the better to enable them to carry on such business to advantage; also, to purchase, take, hold, occupy, possess and enjoy any such lands, tenements and hereditaments, in the counties of Hartford, New Haven and Litchfield as shall be necessary for the views and purposes of said corporation; also, to take and hold a lease or leases of mining privileges, and all of said property to sell and dispose of at pleasure; also, to sue and be sued, plead and be impleaded, defend and be defended, answer and be answered unto, in any court of record or elsewhere, and said corporation may have and use a common seal, and may alter the same at their pleasure.

SEC. 2. The capital stock of said corporation shall not exceed five hundred thousand dollars, and a share of said stock shall be one hundred dollars, and shall be deemed and considered per sonal estate, and be transferable only on the books of said company in such form as the directors of said company shall prescribe; and said company shall at all times have a lien upon all the stock or property of the members of said corporation invested therein for all debts due from them to said company.

SEC. 3. The stock, property and affairs of the corporation shall be managed by not less than three nor more than nine directors, one of whom they shall appoint their president, who shall hold their offices for one year;—which directors shall be stockholders and shall be annually elected at such time and place as the regulations of said corporation shall prescribe, a majority of the directors shall, on all occasions when met, constitute a board for the transaction of business, and a majority of the stockholders present, at any legal meeting, shall be capable of transacting the business of said meeting, each share entitling the owner thereof to one vote, and James Brown, Horatio Allen, Robert M Stratton, Edward C. Delevan, Erastus Corning and John T. Norton, shall be the first directors of said corporation

SEC. 4 The president and directors for the time being or a major part of them, shall have power to fill any vacancy which may happen in their board by death, resignation or otherwise, for the current year, and to appoint and employ, from time to time, a secretary treasurer, and such other officers, mechanics and laborers as they may think proper for the transaction of the business and concerns of the said company and also to make and establish such by-laws, rules and regulations as they shall think expedient for the better management of the concerns of said corporation and the same to alter and repeal, *provided always*, that such by-laws, rules and regulations be not inconsistent with the laws of this state or of the United States

SEC. 5 Said directors shall and may as often as the interest of the stockholders shall require, and the affairs of said company will permit, declare a dividend or dividends of profit on each share, which shall be paid by the treasurer of said company

SEC 6 If it shall so happen that an election of directors should not take place in any year at the annual meeting of the corporation, the said corporation shall not for that reason be dissolved, but such election may be held thereafter on any convenient day within one year, to be fixed on by the directors, they previously giving public notice thereof.

Sec. 7. The books of said company containing their accounts, shall at all reasonable times be open for the inspection of any of the stockholders of said company, and as often as once in each year, a statement of the accounts of said company shall be made by order of the directors; and the secretary of said company shall once in each year certify the amount of stock paid in, the names of the stockholders, and the amount of stock held by each stockholder which certificate of the secretary of the company shall be filed in the office of the Secretary of the State of Connecticut.

Sec. 8. The directors may call in the subscriptions to the capital stock by installments in such proportions and at such times and places as they may think proper, giving such notice thereof as the by laws and regulations of said company shall prescribe, and in case any stockholder shall neglect or refuse payment of such installment or installments for the term of sixty days after the same shall become due and payable, and after he, she, or they have been notified thereof, such negligent stockholder or stockholders shall forfeit to said company all his, her, or their previous installments, together with all his, her, or their rights and interest whatever in said stock.

Sec. 9. For debts which may at any time be due from said company, the stockholders thereof shall not be responsible in their private capacity, but the property and estate of said corporation only shall be liable.

Sec. 10. *Provided*, that nothing contained in this Act shall be construed to authorize and empower the said corporation to use their funds for any banking transactions—*and also provided*, that said company, within twelve months from the passing of this act, shall lodge a certificate with the town clerk of the town of Bristol in said Hartford county, containing the amount of capital stock actually paid in and belonging to said company, and the amount of the capital stock, thus certified, shall not be withdrawn so as to reduce the same below the amount stated in said certificate. *Provided also,* if any part of the capital stock paid in and certified shall be withdrawn without the consent of the General Assembly, the directors ordering, causing, or allowing such withdrawal or reduction, shall be liable, jointly and severally, as traders in company, in case of the insolvency of said corporation at any period afterwards, for all debts owing by said corporation at the time of, or subsequently to the reduction or diminution of the capital aforesaid.

SEC. 11. *And also provided,* That this grant shall be subject to be altered, amended, or repealed, at the pleasure of the General Assembly.

GENERAL ASSEMBLY, MAY SESSION, 1855

Resolved by this Assembly,

SEC. 1 That modified by the amendments hereinafter provided, the Act of 1849, incorporating 'The Bristol Mining Company,' is hereby declared to be in full force and virtue, (any doubts which may have arisen to the contrary notwithstanding,) and is hereby revived and reenacted and shall have the same effect as if the same had been enacted for the first time present session.

SEC. 2 The name of George F Allen is hereby substituted for the name of John T Norton, in sections 1 and 3 of said Act.

SEC. 3 Said corporation is hereby authorized to divide its capital stock into shares of fifty dollars each

SEC. 4 Said corporation is hereby authorized to increase its capital stock, from time to time, to an amount not exceeding the sum of two hundred and fifty thousand dollars over and above the amount of capital stock to which said corporation is limited by the second section of said Act

SEC. 5 *Resolved further,* That this Act may be altered, amended, or repealed, at the pleasure of the General Assembly and shall take effect from the day of its passage

STATE OF CONNECTICUT, ss.
OFFICE OF THE SECRETARY OF STATE

I hereby certify that the foregoing is a true copy of record in this Office

In testimony of which I have set my hand and affixed the seal of said State at Hartford, this 4th day of September A D 1855

[L. S.]   N D SPERRY, *Secretary of State*

CPSIA information can be obtained at www.ICGtesting.com
Printed in the USA
BVOW031306080512